Linux:

The Ultimate Beginner's Guide

Lee Maxwell

TABLE OF CONTENT

Introduction

I want to thank you and congratulate you for downloading the book, *"Linux: The Ultimate Beginner's Guide"*.

This book contains proven steps and strategies on "LINUX"... Linux is the best-known and most-utilized open source working framework. As a working framework, Linux is programming that sits underneath the greater part of the other programming on a PC, getting demands from those projects and transferring these solicitations to the PC's e*q*uipment.

For the reasons for this page, we utilize the expression "Linux" to allude to the Linux portion, additionally the arrangement of projects, devices, and administrations that are ordinarily packaged together with the Linux bit to give the greater part of the important segments of a completely utilitarian working framework. A few people, especially individuals from the Free Software Foundation, allude to this accumulation as GNU/Linux, in light of the fact that a number of the devices included are GNU segments. Be that as it may, not all Linux establishments utilize GNU segments as a piece of their working framework. Android, for instance, utilizes a Linux bit however depends next to no on GNU devices.

Thanks again for downloading this book, I hope you enjoy it!

Chapter 1

What is Linux?

Linux is the best-known and most-utilized open source working framework. As a working framework, Linux is programming that sits underneath the greater part of the other programming on a PC, getting demands from those projects and transferring these solicitations to the PC's equipment.

For the reasons for this page, we utilize the expression "Linux" to allude to the Linux portion, additionally the arrangement of projects, devices, and administrations that are ordinarily packaged together with the Linux bit to give the greater part of the important segments of a completely utilitarian working framework. A few people, especially individuals from the Free Software Foundation, allude to this accumulation as GNU/Linux, in light of the fact that a number of the devices included are GNU segments. Be that as it may, not all Linux establishments utilize GNU segments as a piece of their working framework. Android, for instance, utilizes a Linux bit however depends next to no on GNU devices.

How does Linux contrast from other working frameworks?

From various perspectives Linux is like other working frameworks you may have utilized some time recently, for example, Windows, OS X, or iOS. Like other working frameworks, Linux has a graphical interface, and sorts of programming you are acclimated to utilizing on other working frameworks, for example, word handling applications, have Linux reciprocals. As a rule, the product's maker may have made a Linux form of a similar program you use on different frameworks. On the off chance that you can utilize a PC or other electronic gadget, you can utilize Linux.

Be that as it may, Linux likewise is not quite the same as other working frameworks in numerous essential ways. Initially, and maybe in particular, Linux is open source programming. The code used to make Linux is free and accessible to the general population to see, alter, and—for clients with the suitable aptitudes—to add to.

Linux is likewise extraordinary in that, in spite of the fact that the center bits of the Linux working framework are for the most part regular, there are numerous conveyances of Linux, which incorporate distinctive programming choices. This implies Linux is extraordinarily adjustable, in light of the fact that not simply applications, for example, word processors and web programs, can be swapped out. Linux clients likewise can pick center parts, for example, which framework shows representation, and other UI segments.

What is the contrast amongst Unix and Linux?

You may have known about Unix, which is a working framework created in the 1970s at Bell Labs by Ken Thompson, Dennis Ritchie, and others. Unix and Linux are comparable from multiple points of view, and truth be told, Linux was initially made to be like Unix. Both have comparative instruments for interfacing with the frameworks, programming apparatuses, filesystem formats, and other key parts. Be that as it may, Unix is not free. Throughout the years, various distinctive working frameworks have been made that endeavored to be "unix-like" or "unix-good," however Linux has been the best, far outperforming its forerunners in fame.

Who utilizes Linux?

You're most likely as of now utilizing Linux, whether you know it or not. Contingent upon which client overview you take a gander at, somewhere around one-and 66% of the pages on the Internet are produced by servers running Linux.

Organizations and people pick Linux for their servers since it is secure, and you can get incredible support from an extensive group of clients, notwithstanding organizations like Canonical, SUSE, and Red Hat, which offer business bolster.

A considerable lot of the gadgets you possess most likely, for example, Android telephones, advanced capacity gadgets, individual video recorders, cameras, wearables, and then some, additionally run Linux. Indeed, even your auto has Linux running in the engine.

Who "claims" Linux?

By righteousness of its open source authorizing, Linux is unreservedly accessible to anybody. In any case, the trademark on the name "Linux" rests with its maker, Linus Torvalds. The source code for Linux is under copyright by its numerous individual creators, and authorized under the GPLv2 permit. Since Linux has such an extensive number of givers from over numerous many years of advancement, reaching every individual creator and motivating them to consent to another permit is essentially unimaginable, with the goal that Linux staying authorized under the GPLv2 in unendingness is everything except guaranteed.

How was Linux made?

Linux was made in 1991 by Linus Torvalds, a then-understudy at the University of Helsinki. Torvalds constructed Linux as a free and open source other option to Minix, another Unix clone that was prevalently utilized as a part of scholastic settings. He initially planned to name it "Freax," yet the manager of the server Torvalds used to disperse the first code named his index "Linux" after a blend of Torvalds' first name and the word Unix, and the name stuck.

How might I add to Linux?

The greater part of the Linux bit is composed in the C programming dialect, with a tiny bit of get together and different dialects sprinkled in. In case you're keen on composing code for the Linux portion itself, a great place to begin is in the Kernel Newbies FAQ, which will clarify a portion of the ideas and procedures you'll need to be acquainted with.

Be that as it may, the Linux people group is substantially more than the piece, and needs commitments from bunches of other individuals other than software engineers. Each appropriation contains hundreds or a large number of projects that can be disseminated alongside it, and each of these projects, and in addition the conveyance itself, require an assortment of individuals and ability sets to make them effective, including:

• Testers to ensure everything deals with various setups of equipment and programming, and to report the bugs when it doesn't.

• Designers to make UIs and design circulated with different projects.

• Writers who can make documentation, how-tos, and other essential content circulated with programming.

• Translators to take projects and documentation from their local dialects and make them available to individuals around the globe.

• Packagers to take programming projects and set up every one of the parts together to ensure they run immaculately in various conveyances.

• Evangelists to get the message out about Linux and open source when all is said in done.

• And obviously engineers to compose the product itself.

How might I begin utilizing Linux?

There's some possibility you're utilizing Linux as of now and don't have any acquaintance with it, yet in the event that you'd get a kick out of the chance to introduce Linux on your home PC to give it a shot, the most straightforward path is to pick a well known circulation that is intended for your stage (for instance, portable PC or tablet gadget) and give it a shot. In spite of the fact that there are various conveyances accessible, the majority of the more seasoned, understood circulations are great decisions for tenderfoots since they have expansive client groups that can answer questions on the off chance that you stall out or can't make sense of things. Prevalent circulations incorporate Debian, Fedora, Mint, and Ubuntu, yet there are numerous others.

Do you require programming aptitudes to learn Linux?

A couple of months prior I took the Introduction to Linux course offered through edX. It's a 18 section course with loads of perusing, a few recordings, and an easygoing level of testing your insight. I expounded on the initial six parts and how the course functions in, What happens when a non-coder tries to learn Linux. In this article, I cover the initial 6 sections of the course, where we start to plunge into the everyday utilization of Linux.

What was secured

The course gives a down to earth manual for "getting around" in Linux, covering probably the most generally utilized summons. In spite of the fact that these subjects are not especially hard to comprehend, and might be predicable for a few clients, newcomers will rapidly get to be distinctly lost without a decent comprehension of their motivation and utilization.

In this segment, I ended up depending intensely on Google, and I thought about whether a portion of the ideas would come all the more normally in the event that I had as of now experienced them in programming courses.

A portion of the subjects we secured included:

- Linux documentation

- file operations and frameworks

- read (r), compose (w), and execute (x)

- What are 'executable doubles'?

- user environment su and sudo

- !! blast

- text editors: with exceptionally definite data on vi and emacs

- local security and passwords

- network operations

• ping

• the charge line: regularly permits clients to perform undertakings more proficiently than the GUI

• wget

Try not to stress if a portion of the things on this rundown look remote to you, as they will be shrouded in the course.

Introducing Linux on my Chromebook

My principle objective in taking the course was to show signs of improvement, abnormal state comprehension of Linux. I didn't need to introduce Linux however needed to, so before I began section 7, I did. I needed to try out a portion of the things I was learning, and 'learning is doing' to an expansive degree.

I found a Lifehacker article that looked snappy and simple to take after. It trained me on the best way to introduce Ubuntu utilizing Crouton.

This was genuinely simple, with a couple hiccups en route, which for me was simply part of getting used to entering charges into the terminal and figuring out how to function with and use Linux. NetSurf was the default web program, so I attempted to introduce Firefox. After a couple of disappointments to dispatch, I understood I required sudo!

At that point I began section 7. The material expressed: "Whether you are an unpracticed client or a veteran, you won't generally know how to utilize different Linux projects and utilities, or what to sort at the summon line." I was support by that as I came, exchanging forward and backward between the material and my Chromebook. At a certain point I got sucked into tweaking and modifying my new Linux setup for 60 minutes before returning to the material. This article helped me alter the text style and introduce programs like Leafpad and Audacious.

Is this a decent course for non-coders?

When all is said in done this was not a course for a non-coder hoping to show signs of improvement, abnormal state comprehension of Linux.

This was a course for maybe a novice developer, or a prepared software engineer less acquainted with Linux. A few sections were very definite and particular. Generally speaking, a fundamental base learning of programming would have been to a great degree accommodating. More than a fundamental comprehension, a base comprehension—like that you would get from taking no less than one, full programming course in your life.

Thus, I think I'll reexamine my announcement. This could be a course for a non-coder, since coding won't not be your normal everyday employment or your leisure activity, but rather it's a course best taken after a prologue to software engineering and programming. Which I plan to take next. Along these lines, I'll make one slight stride back to make up for lost time a bit. At that point, I need to dispatch forward again with this Linux Academy course on the best way to introduce and modify Linux as your desktop.

In case you're a non-coder intrigued by taking this course, do it. Why not? It's free, professionally done (by the Linux Foundation), and now and then when you bounce in the profound end you figure out how to swim speedier. I kind of went at it like I recognized what was going on and what the material was discussing notwithstanding when I just half caught on. That helped me in two ways. For one, to some degree you have to *q*uite recently get past new material. You can backtrack, rehash, and retake tests, however when energy truly should be on your side, you must figure out how to simply continue onward and achieve the end. Since I continued moving, as well, I could gather a few pearls from the boundless scene of for the most part new data. For the things I did perceive and the couple of things I had done some time recently, they seemed well and good.

Test drive Linux with only a glimmer drive

Possibly you've found out about Linux and are charmed by it. So captivated that you need to try it out. In any case, you won't not know where to start.

You've presumably done a touch of research on the web and have keep running crosswise over terms like double booting and virtualization. Those terms may make no difference to you, and you're certainly not prepared to give up the working framework that you're at present utilizing to try Linux out. So what would you be able to do?

On the off chance that you have a USB streak drive lying around, you can test drive Linux by making a live USB. It's a USB streak drive that contains a working framework that can begin from the glimmer drive. It doesn't take much specialized capacity to make one. How about we investigate how to do that and how to run Linux utilizing a live USB.

Chapter 2

What you'll re*q*uire

Beside a desktop or tablet phone, require:

• A clear USB streak drive—ideally one that has a limit of 4 GB or more.

• An ISO picture (a document of the substance of a hard circle) of the Linux dispersion that you need to attempt. More about this in a minute.

• An application called Unetbootin, an open source instrument, cross stage device that makes a live USB. You don't should run Linux to utilize it. In the guidelines that underneath, I'm running Unetbootin on a MacBook.

Getting the chance to work

Connect your blaze drive to a USB port on your PC and after that start up Unetbootin. You'll be requested the secret key that you use to sign into your PC.

Keep in mind the ISO picture that was specified a couple of minutes prior? There are two ways you can get one: either by downloading it from the site of the Linux dissemination that you need to attempt, or by having Unetbootin download it for you. To do that last mentioned, click Select Distribution at the highest point of the window, pick the conveyance that you need to download, and after that snap Select Version to choose the form of the dispersion that you need to attempt.

On the other hand, you can download the dissemination yourself. For the most part, the Linux dispersions that I need to attempt aren't in the rundown. On the off chance that you go the second course, click Disk picture and afterward tap the catch to look for the .iso record that you downloaded.

See the Space used to protect records crosswise over reboots (Ubuntu just) choice? In case you're trying Ubuntu or one of its subordinates (like Lubuntu or Xubuntu), you can set aside a couple of megabytes of space on your blaze drive to spare records like web program bookmarks or reports that you make. When you stack Ubuntu from the blaze drive once more, you can reuse those documents.

Once the ISO picture is stacked, click OK. It takes anyplace from a few minutes to 10 minutes for Unetbootin to make the live USB.

Trying out the live USB

This is the indicate where you have grasp your internal nerd a bit. Not excessively, but rather you will take a look into the innards of your PC by going into the BIOS. Your PC's BIOS begins different bits of equipment and controls where the PC's working framework begins, or boots, from.

The BIOS normally searches for the working framework in a specific order (or something like it): hard drive, then CD-ROM or DVD drive, and afterward an outside drive. You'll need to change that request so that the outside drive (for this situation, your live USB) is the one that the BIOS checks first.

To do that, restart your PC with the blaze drive connected to a USB port. When you see the message Press F2 to enter setup, do only that. On a few PCs, the key may be F10.

In the BIOS, utilize the correct bolt key on your console to explore to the Boot menu. You'll see a rundown of drives on your PC. Utilize the down bolt key on your console to explore to the thing marked USB HDD and afterward press F6 to move that thing to the highest priority on the rundown.

Once you've done that, press F10 to spare the progressions. You'll be kicked out of the BIOS and your PC will start up. After a short measure of time, you'll be given a menu posting the alternatives for beginning the Linux conveyance you're experimenting with. Select Run without introducing (or the menu thing nearest to it).

Once the desktop loads, you can interface with a remote or wired system, peruse the web, and give the pre-introduced programming a spin. You can likewise verify whether, for instance, your printer or scanner works with the Linux conveyance you're trying. In the event that you outrageously need to you can likewise fiddle at the order line.

What's in store

Contingent upon the Linux appropriation you're trying and the speed of the glimmer drive you're utilizing, the working framework may take more time to load and it may run a bit slower than it would on the off chance that it was introduced on your hard drive.

Also, you'll just have the essential programming that the Linux dispersion packs out of the case. You by and large get a web program, a word processor, a content tool, a media player, a picture viewer, and an arrangement of utilities. That ought to be sufficient to give you a vibe for what it resembles to utilize Linux.

On the off chance that you conclude that you like utilizing Linux, you can introduce it from the glimmer drive by double tapping on the installer.

8 Linux record directors to attempt

A standout amongst the most widely recognized authoritative errands that end clients and heads alike need to perform is document administration. Overseeing records can expend a noteworthy part of your time. Finding documents, figuring out which records and envelopes (catalogs) are taking the most plate space, erasing records, moving records, and just opening documents for use in an application are probably the most fundamental—yet visit—errands we do as PC clients. Record administration projects are devices that are proposed to streamline and rearrange those essential errands.

Numerous decisions

Many individuals aren't mindful of the wide cluster of decisions accessible in document supervisors, nor do they understand the full abilities of the ones they do think about. Similarly as with each part of Linux, there are numerous alternatives accessible for record administrators. The most widely recognized ones gave by my most loved conveyance, Fedora, are:

• Midnight Commander

• Konqueror

• Dolphin

- Krusader

- Nautilus

- Thunar

- PCmanFM

- XFE

I have utilized each of these at different circumstances for different reasons and they all have *q*ualities to suggest them. Running from extremely easy to highlight pressed, there is a record supervisor accessible that will address your issues. Midnight Commander and Krusader are my most loved document directors, and I utilize both much of the time, however I additionally end up utilizing Dolphin and Konqueror.

This article takes a gander at each of the document chiefs recorded above and thinks about a couple of their primary elements. Tragically, there is insufficient space to do each of these document supervisors e*q*uity. I want to have some future articles that give a more definite take a gander at a few of these intense devices.

Each of these document supervisors is configurable, with Krusader and Konqueror being the most configurable of the GUI-based record chiefs. Midnight authority, the solitary content based record supervisor, is additionally very configurable.

None of the record directors look as a matter of course as they do in this archive. I have designed them to resemble this on my frameworks. Aside from Midnight Commander, the hues are overseen in the "Application Appearance" area of the KDE System Settings application and are not configurable inside the applications themselves.

Default File Manager

Like most Linux circulations, Fedora has a default document administrator, which is as of now Dolphin. The Linux desktop ordinarily has a symbol that resembles a little house—that is your home catalog/envelope. Tap on the Home symbol and the default record administrator opens with your home index as the PWD, or Present Working Directory. In current discharges that utilization KDE 4.1 or over, the Home symbol is situated in the Desktop Folder alongside the Trash symbol, as demonstrated as follows.

In KDE, the default document director can be changed utilizing System Settings > Default Applications > File Manager.

Midnight Commander

Midnight Commander is a content based Command Line Interface (CLI) program. It is especially helpful when a GUI is not accessible, but rather can likewise be utilized as an essential record supervisor in a terminal session notwithstanding when you are utilizing a GUI. I utilize Midnight Commander regularly in light of the fact that I frequently need to associate with neighborhood and remote Linux PCs utilizing the CLI. It can be utilized with any of the basic shells and remote terminals through SSH.

You can begin Midnight Commander from the CLI with the mc summon. The above picture indicates Midnight Commander in one tab of the Konsole program. The UI for Midnight Commander is two content mode sheets, left and right, which every show the substance of a catalog. The highest point of every sheet shows the name of the present index for that sheet. Route is proficient with the bolt and tab keys. The Enter key can be utilized to enter a highlighted index.

Along the extremely top of the Midnight Commander interface is a menu bar containing menu things for arranging Midnight Commander, the left and right sheets, and for issuing different document orders. The base part of the interface shows data about the record or index highlighted in every sheet, a clue include and a line of capacity key marks; you can essentially press the capacity key on your console that relates to the capacity you need to perform. Between the indication line and the capacity keys is an order line.

Chapter 3

Krusader

Krusader is an uncommon document director that is designed according to Midnight Commander. It utilizes a comparable two-sheet interface, however it's graphical rather than content based. Krusader gives many elements that upgrade its usefulness as a record supervisor. Krusader permits you to utilize a similar console route and order structure as Midnight Commander, furthermore permits you to utilize the mouse or trackball to explore and play out the greater part of the standard simplified operations you would expect on documents.

The essential UI for Krusader, much like that of Midnight Commander, is two content mode sheets—left and right—which every show the substance of a registry. The highest point of every sheet contains the name of the present catalog for that sheet. What's more, tabs can be opened for every sheet and an alternate catalog can be open in every tab. Route is expert with the bolt and tab keys or the mouse. The Enter key can be utilized to enter a highlighted index.

Every tab and sheet can be arranged to show documents in one of two unique Modes. In the representation above, documents are shown in the point by point see that—notwithstanding the record name and a symbol or see—demonstrates the record estimate, the date it was last altered, the proprietor, and the record consents.

Along the extremely top of the Krusader GUI are a menu bar and toolbar containing menu things for arranging Krusader and overseeing documents. The base bit of the interface shows a line of capacity key names; you can basically press the capacity key on your console that compares to the capacity you need to perform. At the base of the interface is an order line.

Krusader consequently spares the present tab and catalog areas and in addition other setup things so you will dependably come back to the last arrangement and set of registries while restarting the application.

Konqueror

Konqueror is another capable and adaptable record director with many components. It has one component that none of the other document supervisors do: it serves as a web program. Simply sort the URL of the site you need to see in the area bar.

The primary concern that separates Konqeuror from the group is the capacity to open various tabs, each of which can have at least one registry route sheets. In the picture underneath, one tab has been isolated into three sheets; one on the left side and two on the privilege. The sidebar at the far left is utilized to give quick route of the whole filesystem.

One thing I especially like about Konqueror is that it gives a magnificent abnormal state perspective of your registry structure, both in the sidebar and in the index boards. This makes it simpler to find and erase records and registry trees that are did not require anymore. It additionally empowers less demanding route and revamping of the registry structure.

The essential UI for Konqueror, much like that of Midnight Commander and Krusader, is content mode sheets that show the substance of a registry. Konqueror, notwithstanding, permits various sheets, and the default single sheet can be part both on a level plane and vertically the same number of times as it bodes well to do as such. Konqueror likewise underpins various tabs (at the highest point of the index sheets this time) and an alternate arrangement of registries can be open in every tab. Route is refined with the bolt and tab keys or the mouse. The Enter key can be utilized to enter a highlighted registry. The Location gadget close to the highest point of the Kon*q*ueror GUI contains the full way of the presently chose sheet.

Every tab and sheet can be designed to show documents in one of two distinct Modes. In the above picture, records are shown in the point by point see which, notwithstanding the document name and a symbol or see, demonstrates the document measure, the date it was last adjusted, the proprietor, and the record consents.

Along the extremely top of the Graphical User Interface are a menu bar and apparatus bar containing menu things for designing Kon*q*ueror and overseeing documents. When you have the tabs and sheets set up the way you need them, you can spare it so Kon*q*ueror will dependably begin with that setup.

Dolphin

Dolphin is especially similar to Konqueror and Krusader. It has two index route sheets and a sidebar that takes into account simple filesystem route. It underpins tabs.

The essential UI for Dolphin can be arranged to be fundamentally the same as Konqueror and Krusader. Utilizing two sheets which every show the substance of an index, it doesn't bolster part the sheets. Route is refined with the bolt and tab keys or the mouse. The Enter key can be utilized to enter a highlighted index. Dolphin additionally bolsters growing the registry trees (organizers) in both the sidebar route sheet and the catalog sheets.

In spite of the fact that Dolphin supports tabs, when restarted it generally returns to the default of one sets of registry sheets that show your home catalog.

Nautilus

Nautilus has a solitary catalog sheet with which to work. It additionally has a sidebar for route. Nautilus is a straightforward, respectable document director that is useful for some tenderfoots because of its straightforwardness. Nautilus is commonly found in frameworks where GNOME is the desktop, yet it can likewise be introduced and utilized with KDE.

The essential UI for Nautilus is genuinely straightforward with a route sidebar and a solitary index window in which to work. It doesn't bolster numerous tabs or part the sheets. Route is refined with the bolt and tab keys or the mouse. The Enter key can be utilized to enter a highlighted registry.

Thunar

Thunar is another lightweight document supervisor. It is so much like Nautilus in the way it looks and works and that there is nothing else to say in regards to it.

PCmanFM

The PCManFM document supervisor is expected to supplant Nautilus and Thunar. Truth be told, in light of the way they look and work so much indistinguishable, they may really share some normal code. These three document supervisors have the least setup choices and all have a similar straightforward interface.

XFE

XFE is one of the all the more fascinating of the record directors as it has an interface all its own and is more adaptable than Nautilus, Thunar, and PCManFM.

XFE might be designed to show maybe a couple catalog sheets, and the route bar is discretionary. It plays out all the normal intuitive capacities, however it requires some manual arrangement to relate the right applications like LibreOffice with particular document sorts. It has a sensible arrangement of setup choices, however no place close to those of Konqueror or Krusader.

XFE is additionally very troublesome about holding its own particular arrangement of "subjects" and has no alternative to utilize the desktop shading plan, symbols, improvements, or gadgets.

Suggestions

I realize that there are other document directors, one of which might be your top pick. Your decision of document chief ought to be the one that works best for you. GNU/Linux gives a few practical decisions and one will doubtlessly address the greater part of your issues. On the off chance that your most loved does not address your issues for a specific undertaking, you can simply utilize the one that does.

These document supervisors are for nothing out of pocket and dispersed under some type of open source permit. All are accessible from regular, trusted vaults for Fedora and CentOS.

I plan to compose some extra articles that cover some of these record administrators in more fine grained detail. If you don't mind leave your remarks to tell me which ones you might want to know more about.

6 reasons individuals with incapacities ought to utilize Linux

Regularly, when issues of availability and assistive innovation are raised among individuals with inabilities, the subjects revolve around the typical issues: How would I be able to manage the cost of this gadget? Is it accessible for me? Will it address my issues? By what means will I get bolster?

Open source arrangements, including any Linux-based working framework, are infrequently, if at any point, considered. The issue isn't with the arrangement; rather, it is a consequence of absence of data and familiarity with FOSS and GNU/Linux in the incapacity group, and even among individuals by and large. Here are six strong reasons individuals with inabilities ought to consider utilizing Linux

Chapter 4

Customization and alteration

Assistive innovation has made some amazing progress from its not really far off past; be that as it may, exclusive gadgets are restricted in their capacity to adjust and adjust to their clients. Few standard arrangements are accessible, and even less are opened, ready to be adjusted at the lower levels. Having the capacity to take existing innovation and adjust it to suit one's needs—as opposed to constraining a man to adjust to the gadget and additionally programming—is a quality of open source programming and Linux, and is critical for the individuals who depend on a gadget to finish what others underestimate each day.

A couple of years back, for instance, I took a shot at a concede extend in the place where I grew up. Part of the venture was to advance netbooks to understudies with inabilities who indicated noteworthy administration potential. One of the understudies truly delighted in utilizing the netbook's webcam to take pictures; be that as it may, the working framework stacked on the gadget utilized content, not pictures, to separate amongst documents and envelopes. Without having the capacity to peruse the way to the organizer where the webcam spared pictures, they were not ready to discover them.

After some exchange, I changed out the working framework for Ubuntu Netbook Remix, which had a simple to-utilize GUI and, all the more essentially, a symbol set that utilized images to distinguish what was contained in the organizers: a filmstrip for recordings, a music note for sound records, a letter for reports, and a square photograph (like a Polaroid) for pictures. That is all it took—a straightforward change in symbols and the obstruction that forestalled full utilize was dispensed with.

Steadiness, dependability, and sturdiness

Whether you depend on a content to-discourse program to speak with others, a gadget that helps the individuals who are visually impaired in route, a discourse to-content application that helps with writing and information, or something else fundamental to your day by day life, the thing you depend on can't be delicate nor effortlessly broken. A steady stage that can survive expanded lengths of uptime without solidifying, bolting up, or slamming is an absolute necessity. A similar bit that is utilized to control the world's servers is an undeniable decision to keep somebody's available gadget running when it's required most.

Similarity with out of date or old equipment

Restrictive assistive innovation gadgets—particularly while tending to more extreme incapacities—regularly keep running on more established, dated equipment. Regardless of the possibility that one can acquire a present form of the product they require, that doesn't generally mean the equipment they possess will have the capacity to run it. Through Linux, in any case, a maturing gadget can be restored, and the individual with an inability won't need to always update their e*q*uipment. This decreases cost, both so as to learn and adjust to new e*q*uipment and in money related cost.

Control and full proprietorship

For future assistive innovation gadgets to be completely open, the product and the gadget being used must be alterable and adjust to the person, rather than driving an adjustment in the individual's capacity to adjust to a capable world. By having admittance to the code, individuals with inabilities can investigate and guarantee that the product they are utilizing is under their control and working for them. This get to likewise decreases issues with protection and security, which is doubly imperative when the gadget one depends upon handles almost the greater part of your touchy information. Without possession and full control, any advantage an assistive innovation gadget gives is obliged and utilized against the organization that created it, unfulfilling the accepted motivation behind its programming. Every one of us need the equipment and programming we paid for to work for us in view of our requests and needs, and individuals with handicaps are the same.

Help from an expansive, universal group

A hefty portion of us know the torment of attempting to get help for a restrictive gadget or program, tending to the telephone and getting just constrained offer assistance. This turns out to be far and away more terrible when attempting to comprehend an issue with an assistive innovation gadget; support is constrained, there are regularly few or no physical retailers that will supplant your gadget, and because of its remarkable, secured setup, there are couple of neighborhood people who can investigate and tackle such issues. When you utilize Linux, the whole Internet is your asset. Discussions, IRC/talk rooms, online recordings and instructional exercises, and more choices are all accessible to guide anybody—from the most tenderfoot of apprentices to experience veterans of the sysadmin world—through almost any trouble. One outstanding favorable position here is that when somebody posts a question or depicts a late cerebral pain on the web, innumerable other individuals find out about it, and some of them might ask a similar question.

Fun

The truth of the matter is, Linux is enjoyable. The excite of forming, embellishment, and altering a framework to individual needs is significant. Indicating others what you've assembled is quite recently piece of it; demonstrating how you did it and how they can too is a fundamental part of the open-source group. Who wouldn't have any desire to be incorporated into that?

The most effective method to do *q*uick, repeatable Linux establishments Ninety-nine percent of people in general has never experienced utilizing a similar PC with both Windows Vista and Linux. Individuals ought to be managed that open door, wouldn't you say? In the event that you have extended information, then you have extended choices for the world. I like extended alternatives.

Chapter 5

Four Linux distros for children

I can see the shine of interest in my six year old niece Shuchi's eyes when she investigates a cell phone or controls the simpleton box with its remote control or turns out to be inventively ruinous with some other electronic gadget. She, similar to a great deal of children her age, love testing.

This interest achieves its pinnacle when she sits before my portable PC or her dad's tablet. A considerable measure of times, in any case, I watch that she is lost in entangled applications that are reasonable just to grown-ups. A working framework that a grown-up utilizations and the framework running it can resemble a monster to a ton of children. These applications are outside the ability to understand of exceptionally youthful children and don't give a perfect (and energetic) prologue to PCs. Futher, grown-ups' portable PCs and tablets don't serve as a decent learning environment for any child (more youthful or more established) who is only onboarding into the universe of figuring. Plus, giving a child a chance to run wild on a PC with an online association can overwhelm for the guardians.

As a major child myself, and an open source programming lover for more than four years now, I like investigating and trying different things with various programming arrangements. Relating to the issue of finding and setting up a perfect framework for my young niece, I found that the open source Linux people group has made specific working frameworks and situations for children. Also, setting up these frameworks is a breeze.

Why ought to kids learn Linux

I have achieved a definitive supposition now in my life that kids ought to be presented to the force of Linux at an opportune time. Two of the reasons are...

For the eventual fate of processing

I as of late read the article, A year of Linux desktop at Westcliff High School, which is a brilliant piece by Stu Jarvis in which Malcolm Moore answers to a question by expressing, "Here is a review that reports in 2000, 97% of registering gadgets had Windows introduced, however now with tablets and telephones, and so on., Windows is just on 20% of figuring gadgets, and in the realm of huge iron, Linux rules. We have practical experience in science and building and need our understudies to go ahead to do incredible things like begin the following Google or crumple the universe at CERN. In those situations, they will surely need to know Linux."

Linux runs the absolute most complex foundations on the planet. For anybody even remotely keen on a vocation in innovation, learning Linux will be a clear resource. Other than that, the selection of Linux is monstrous and omnipresent. Consider this:

- Linux powers worldwide space stations

- Linux powers the innovation in new autos like Tesla and Cadillac

- Linux powers airport regulation frameworks

- Google, Facebook, Twitter, all utilization Linux

- 9 out of 10 supercomputers on the planet keep running on Linux

There is a sane reason that activities like One Laptop for each Child, which as I would see it is a standout amongst the most intense projects today that is attempting to connect the computerized isolate, utilize Linux based frameworks.

For customization and assortment

Learning at an early age can be best upgraded in a domain that supports investigation. There is no other working framework that offers such assortment and self-sufficiency to redo the framework in view of particular needs like Linux. Like toys and garments for children, the Linux people group has created particular working frameworks that can offer them a fun learning environment. I trust that to help interest in children, it is vital to make a set up that gives them a sentiment ponder.

Projects to show kids Linux

There are a wide range of assortments of situations that the Linux people group has intended for the kids, and I haven't yet investigated them all, however of the ones I did, you ought to have the capacity to locate an extraordinary answer for educating a child you think about Linux and figuring.

Qimo for children is a Ubuntu-based dispersion composed particularly for youngsters. The working framework comes pre-introduced with a great deal of instructive applications for kids ages 3 years and more seasoned. It accompanies GCompris, a flawless suite for youngsters matured 3 to 10 years. It comprises of more than 100 instructive diversions that shows essential PC utilize, perusing, craftsmanship history, reading a clock, and drawing pictures, and in addition Childs Play, an accumulation of memory-building recreations.

Something I like best about this conveyance is that it utilizes XFCE desktop , which is a lightweight desktop that can be introduced on more established machines. The equipment necessities are low and it is ludicrously simple to repurpose an old portable PC or a desktop framework. We had an old PC at home, and Qimo revived it. This working framework was my decision for my niece in view of its straightforward tyke agreeable toon desktop and grouping of instructive applications.

Sugar was intended for the One Laptop for every Child program. It is a simple to utilize and kid-accommodating working framework. Kids who cherish investigating will make sense of things rapidly in this environment, regardless of the possibility that they can't read or compose yet.

From Sugar Labs:

Data is about things; learning is about verbs. The Sugar interface, in its takeoff from the desktop analogy for processing, is the main genuine endeavor to make a UI that depends on both subjective and social constructivism: learners ought to take part in valid investigation and joint effort. It depends on three extremely basic standards about what makes us human.

Ubermix is broadly utilized as a part of schools. The framework was intended to store client information and programming in seperate segments. Along these lines, on the off chance that the PC glitches, the client can wipe out the working framework and resotre new duplicates rapidly. From Ubermix author, Jim Klein, in an Opensource.com meet:

Ubermix comes pre-stacked with various applications for training, efficiency, plan, programming, Internet, and sight and sound development. Instruction situated applications like Celestia, Stellarium, Scratch, VirtualLab Microscope, Geogebra, iGNUit, and Klavaro, and in addition instructive amusements like TuxMath, TuxTyping, gMult, and Numpty Physics all carry with them a lot of chances to learn.

Web applications we as a whole know and love, as Firefox, Thunderbird, Chrome, Google Earth, and Skype are all there. Normal profitability applications like LibreOffice, NitroTasks, Planner Project Management, VYM (View Your Mind), and Zim Desktop Wiki are as well. Kids intrigued by configuration will discover the GIMP, Inkscape, Scribus, Dia, Agave, and even TuxPaint for the more youthful ones. What's more, applications like Audacity, Openshot, Pencil, and ffDiaporama round out the media offerings. These, and some more, make Ubermix a capable launchpad for understudy inventiveness and learning.

Formally the Ubuntu Education Edition, Edubuntu was produced in a joint effort with instructors and educators. It inserts an assortment of instructive projects and a reasonable learning environment. Leverage to it is access to the Ubuntu programming vault. The training group has broadly utilized this working framework as a part of schools and associations to give an advanced learning environment to their understudies. It's an incredible working framework to educate more seasoned kids about Linux; it can have a more extreme expectation to absorb information in contrast with Qimo and Sugar.

The present condition of video altering for Linux

I regularly solicit myself what the present state from video altering is for nothing and open source programming (FOSS). Here are my contemplations.

I've spent numerous years in the visual impacts (VFX) industry from the viewpoint of being either a craftsman, printer, video supervisor, or frameworks build. (I've even got film creds on IMDB!) previously, I had the joy of cutting on, preparing individuals on, setting up, and supporting Avid Media Composer, the cream of the harvest of expert ongoing video altering instruments for film and TV alike—in any event before things like Final Cut Pro and Adobe Premiere got to be distinctly sufficiently valuable to experts.

In the VFX business these three devices are utilized widely among studios for cutting video and film and are both exceptionally easy to use for noobs and experts alike and also can be pushed extremely far in the hands of master craftsmen. The VFX business has generally of the most recent 30 years been dependent on Mac and PC for video altering, principally on the grounds that the greater part of the Linux-based FOSS instruments have been not as much as extraordinary. This is a disgrace since the majority of the best 3D and 2D apparatuses, other than video, are settled in the Linux environment and perform best there. The absence of better than average video altering devices on Linux keeps each VFX studio from turning into a Linux-just shop.

That being said, there are a few steps being made to extension this crevice, as I found in the course of the most recent couple of weeks. They are not Hollywood huge, creation prepared walks but rather they are sufficiently helpful for what I have to do which is fundamentally a bundle of assemble preparing and demo recordings as Senior Systems Engineer for Red Hat's Systems Engineering EngOps group.

I've introduced and tried various apparatuses before beating my dread of figuring out how to alter video in Blender. (When I initially took a gander at it, the program appeared to be convoluted.) So, here's a record of the instruments I took a gander at and what I contemplated them. Give me a chance to qualify this by telling you that I'm right now running Fedora 21, KDE, and Gnome (since I can't choose which to stay with) on a Lenovo T440s with a VGA good controller: Intel Corporation Haswell-ULT Integrated Graphics Controller (thus, no accellerated openGL tragically). I moved toward this as I would on the off chance that I was a restless craftsman attempting to discover

THE instrument for the occupation, with no time for messing about for practically zero outcomes.

Pitivi

Pitivi was prescribed to me, so it was the primary application I experimented with. It's composed in Python, so I thought possibly I can mess around with scripting this since I have a particular thing I'd get a kick out of the chance to do with overlaying timecode over the video in light of the edge check demonstrating genuine section of time paying little heed to the slices made to the clasp. (It's a demo thing.) It looked extraordinary and proficient esque, practically Avid/debut like. Along these lines, I got a video cut... furthermore, CRASH! I opened it once more, got a clasp, no crash, so that is incredible. I included another video track... what's more, CRASH! I attempted no less than 15 more circumstances before abandoning it. Also, it's a disgrace, since it would appear that it can possibly be easy to utilize and not excessively flashy.

I'll attempt again when variant 1.0 is discharged. Regularly, I continue on with beta variants since I've been included with beta testing programming the greater part of my expert life, yet this was baffling and I wasn't getting anyplace.

OpenShot

For OpenShot: Open it, check. Acquire video, check. Cut video into course of events, check. Playback video, check. Include a title and hit render, then I held up... also, held up... what's more, held up. At that point, I checked htop, and nothing happening except for I couldn't counterbalance of the render. CRASHH!! Gee golly.

Things being what they are, my take was that perhaps this one can carry out the employment on the off chance that you don't need titles? It's free shut source contender, so it might potentially be more helpful? I don't have the foggiest idea, however I proceeded onward.

Lightworks

With Lightworks, I thought: now we're talking. Lightworks had an expansive influence in the expert video showcase around 10 years prior and was utilized by numerous PC based studios. It has cut some truly cool movies en route and was extremely costly then as I review. In this way, nowadays they have discharged a free form for all stages. This form gives all of you the simple things that you may need, and there's a RPM or deb download accessible. It introduced without issues, then when I double tapped the symbol, nothing happened. No OpenGL, no video, no worky.

Might someone be able to give this a shot and let me know what it resembles? Alternately, in case you're feeling liberal, toss me a clever tablet with no less than a Nvidia 870M in it please.

Avidemux

For Avidemux, I introduced it and opened it. Are individuals utilizing this for altering? I took a gander at this as I've seen such a large number of different writeups say this as a proofreader which it most definately isn't. I proceeded onward.

Cinelerra

For Cinelerra, I attempted to download it and found the landing page had no download connect (at the time). I noticed that the group there appears to be exceptionally centered around the Ubuntu client. At that point, I downloaded, extricated, and opened it. I got some video, hit the flashy, huge green tick to acknowledge the import, hit play, and found that it didn't work. Bummer.

KDEnlive

KDEnlive is a moderately new disclosure for me. I introduced it, opened it, set out a few tracks, and cut with my "industry standard" console alternate routes. All appeared to be entirely smooth. Along these lines, then I overlayed the end of one video over the begin of another video track with the goal that I could apply a move, however I couldn't discover any. The rundown of moves was uncovered. Gee, possibly I need to do a reversal and discover why this is.

Along these lines, I'll report back later on this.

Blender

When I got to Blender, I was truly beginning to get dampened. I've taken a gander at Blender in the past yet it was an entirely unexpected worldview than anything I had utilized before professionally. For a begin, the keys we as a whole off-base. Be that as it may, I was back and not going to be vanquished. I scanned YouTube for something to help, something that wouldn't take me 365 days to experience the fundamentals.

Here's a rundown of a couple that I discovered helpful. Also, after around 30 mins of watching, I began.

I imported the video cuts that I required, check. I set out the primary video track, check. I played the clasp back in the player/viewer, check. I was begining to get energized. I began chopping my 45 minute clasp down to 5 minutes. Blender has markers: amazing! Cutting long clasps without markers is a pointless activity. Enthusiastic began the marker pattern and it was a gift from heaven. By utilizing markers with the "m" key you can begin to delineate continuous, while you're watching, where you need the slices to happen. Also, once you're done viewing through, you can skip to every marker and make a cut. You can then non-ruinously erase the clasps that you simply cut. You can then naturally close the hole between each of the cuts so you're not screwing around attempting to arrange the closures of each back to back clasp.

Making moves was truly straightforward as well and helped me to remember utilizing Adobe Premiere. There are some "ordinary" moves as well, ones that you would hope to see on a film or TV dramatization, as opposed to only the "fractal twirl over blur back air pocket" move that the greater part of alternate applications appear to love.

Another pleasant thing about Blender is that the sound can be unlinked from the video. There are many utilizations for this, and I was cheerful to see that I could do it so effectively. The following thing I attempted was titling. You can go the 2D or 3D course. I picked the 3D course as this can give you a great deal more adaptability for reuse. In this way, I overlayed this over the video flawlessly, and after that I picked the configuration and size that I needed to render out with, and hit the GO catch. It rendered out quick and impeccably.

Who helps your Linux conveyance run easily?

The general population in the background who work enthusiastically to make your Linux dissemination run easily are the packagers. Most by far of Linux packagers are volunteers who commit their nighttimes and ends of the week to make and keep up the riggings of the Linux conveyances they cherish.

The Linux biological system is flourishing with various dispersions. They fulfill diverse gatherings of people, needs, and styles. They go from sorts that are:

• secure and reasonable for military and budgetary applications (RHEL)

• bleeding edge and element (Fedora)

• universal (Debian)

• educational (Edubuntu)

• for the specialist (Raspbian)

- for the media craftsman (Ubuntu Studio)

- for the agreeable client (Mint)

- for the desktop application and cloud (Ubuntu)

- simple and lightweighted (Arch)

- faithfully worked from source code (Gentoo)

furthermore, continues going for several different circulations that are consistently developing.

In every one of the cases, the Linux dispersions are conglomerating free and open source bundles, arranging them and consolidating them in a way that guarantee their legitimate aggregate conduct. Because of all that setup and testing, adopters of Linux conveyances have the true serenity of essentially introducing a bundle (a given application) and having the certainty that it will work pleasantly with alternate bundles as of now introduced in the framework.

The "enchantment mythical people" off camera who work indefatigably to make this work easily are the packagers. Most by far of Linux packagers are volunteers who commit their nighttimes and ends of the week to make and keep up the riggings of the Linux conveyances they adore.

Back in February 2012, I had the fortunes of being the primary learner of the Debian Maintainer of the Month (MoM) program, began by Andreas Tille. The objective of the MoM program is to teach and prepare new packagers for the Debian dissemination by blending students with coaches and doing the preparation while bundling another genuine application. The program has every one of the elements for adjusting a fascinating, testing, and compensating assignment.

Amid my preparation, we figured out how to bundle fis-gtm, the open source execution of M/MUMPS that is of extraordinary significance for the environment of open source Electronic Health Records frameworks. The fis-gtm bundle has simply been acknowledged in the Debian unsteady dissemination.

Experiencing the preparation was educational. I took in a lot of exceptionally helpful apparatuses and practices, that from that point forward I keep on using day by day. From the best possible utilization of GPG keys, to chroot control and remote screen imparting to tmux. The joint effort environment was all around portrayed by Andreas Tille as: "Getting up in the morning to understand that somebody in another mainland has effectively tackled for you the issue that had you stuck the previous evening."

In perfect conditions, a Linux packager works intimately with the designers of the upstream bundle in a manner that new arrivals of the bundle can be adjusted rapidly to be incorporated into the following arrival of that Linux dissemination. As a rule, the way toward bundling reveals issues with the bundle that require the upstream designers to roll out improvements and changes. A packager additionally works in close coordination with different packagers in a similar Linux dispersion on the grounds that many bundles have conditions on different bundles or give administrations to different bundles, making it key that the group of packagers arrange their overhauls to guarantee the consistency of the last Linux appropriation.

As Linux clients, it is regularly simple to overlook (slight?) how much work goes into the creation and support of a Linux appropriation.

Turning into a Linux packager is a phenomenal approach to find out about programming improvement, quality control, extend administration, and programming support in a situation of enthusiastic people who profoundly think about the yield of their work. This is an ordeal every single youthful engineer ought to have.

In the wake of having scholarly the ropes of Linux bundling, and having seen direct the commitment of this group, I built up a lot of regard and thankfulness for their work. Presently, every time I introduce a bundle, whether it is from the order line with.

Conclusion

Thank you again for downloading this book!

I hope this book was able to help you to BE ABLE to UNDERSTAND Linux

Finally, if you enjoyed this book, then I'd like to ask you for a favor, would you be kind enough to leave a review for this book on Amazon? It'd be greatly appreciated!

Thank you and good luck!

I truly do appreciate it!

Best Wishes,

Lee Maxwell